BRAZILIAN JUJUTSU
SIDE-MOUNT TECHNIQUES
by Joe Moreira
with Daniel Darrow

D1475160

BRAZILIAN JUJUTSU
SIDE-MOUNT TECHNIQUES
by Joe Moreira
with Daniel Darrow

Edited by Raymond Horwitz
and Edward Pollard

Photography by Greg Wetzel

Graphic Design by John Bodine

Technique Photo Partners:
Paulo Gazze Jr. and Ashot Petrossian

©2004 Black Belt Communications LLC
All Rights Reserved
Printed in the United States of America
Library of Congress Control Number: 2004111634
ISBN 0-89750-145-4

Third printing 2005

WARNING

BLACK BELT BOOKS

A Division of **OHARA** 🏠 **PUBLICATIONS, INC.**

World Leader in Martial Arts Publications

ABOUT THE AUTHOR

Born José Carlos Moreira on July 3, 1961, inside a taxi in front of a Rio de Janeiro hospital, Brazilian *jujutsu* legend Joe Moreira faced difficulties right from the start. His dark skin and blond hair prompted the affectionate nickname of *"Macaco."* By age five, Moreira's older brother, Marcos, influenced the youngster to start fighting in judo. His first title for the Gama Filho University team was won by age six. Around that time he began his jujutsu career under the tutelage of Mauricio LaCerda. At age nine, he began training in jujutsu at the school of the legendary Carlson and Rolls Gracie, where he was taught mainly by Reyson Gracie and Pinduka. Across the street there was another studio owned and operated by Reylson Gracie, nephew and student of the master, Helio Gracie. A chance visit to the studio resulted in Moreira spending the next 15 years under the tutelage of Reylson, who took a liking to the young fighter's style and groomed him to become an instructor. During this period with Master Reylson, Moreira also learned to produce tournaments and championships. This would later help him to organize one of the most important jujutsu tournaments in Brazil, including the first international Brazilian jujutsu event, Atlântico Sul.

Another respected jujutsu master, Francisco Mansour, awarded Moreira his black belt in 1984. By competing in the most important jujutsu tournaments of the 1980s, such as Copa Company, Copa Lightining Bolt and Copa Cantão, Moreira's collection of titles grew. His participation in such events garnered Moreira respect and recognition as one of the toughest fighters of his time.

Around that time, the Gracie family was always looking for tough opponents to take on the undefeated Rickson Gracie. It wasn't long before Moreira accepted the challenge to face his idol *twice* in the same competition (weight-category final and absolute) despite not having good partners with whom to train. Although he submitted in both matches, Moreira gave the jujutsu legend something he was not used to: a tough fight. Following these bouts, a great friendship evolved between the two fighters.

By 1986, Moreira was a black belt in both judo and Brazilian jujutsu. The next step in his evolution came in the form of internships at Terry University, in Japan, and at Kobukan Academy, the traditional judo academy established by judo founder Jigoro Kano. After four months of training with the Japanese Olympic team and completing a course with more than 1,000 black belt students, Moreira became vice champ in an international tournament: the Judo World Cup.

After a year of invaluable training in Japan, Moreira returned to his Brazilian academy in Rio de Janeiro and produced his first tournament: the Atlântico Sul Cup, which saw the debut of world names such as Ryan, Renzo and Ralph Gracie, SHOOTO welterweight champion Vitor "Shaolin" Ribeiro, UFC veteran Jorge Patino, Antonio Schembri and Márcio Feitosa, Cleber Luciano, Wander Braga, Wallid Ishmael, Jean Jacque Machado, Fabio Gurgel, Murilo Bustamante, Mario Sperry, Alan Goes, Mario Sperry, Liborio, De la Riva and others who helped to establish it as a premier tournament. Nine Atlântico Sul Cup events were held between 1986 and 1994, produced with the help of his partners and friends, Cláudio Franca (Cláudio Franca Brazilian Jiu-Jitsu in Santa Cruz, California) and Marcus Vinícius (owner of the Beverly Hills Jiu-Jitsu Club).

In the early 1990s, an invitation from Reylson Gracie prompted Moreira to sell all of his possessions in Brazil and travel to the United States to be a Brazilian jujutsu instructor. "He promised me everything," Moreira remembers, "but when I got there, it was pretty different." Because of some financial disagreements, he decided to go it alone and forge his own path.

After two difficult months in the United States—and despite not speaking a word of English—Moreira teamed up with entrepreneur Cab Garrett to build his first gym, Joe Moreira Jiu-Jitsu de Brazil, in Irvine, California. During his eight-year partnership with Garrett, Moreira opened 30 branches of the school across the country.

Moreira also founded the United States Federation of Brazilian Jiu-Jitsu and played a major role in the dissemination of the art in America. As president of the federation, he created the first international Brazilian jujutsu tournament, the Joe Moreira Cup, and organized the first edition of the Pan-American Jiu-Jitsu Tournament with Carlos Gracie, president of the Brazilian Jiu-Jitsu Confederation. Those events launched the first top representatives of Brazilian jujutsu in America—names like B.J. Penn, Garth Taylor, Egan Inoue, Mark Kompayneyets, Chris Brennan, Eddie Bravo, Javier Vazquez, Ricco Rodriguez and many others that later transformed the United States into the second jujutsu power of the world.

Even while being involved with his U.S. jujutsu organization, Moreira kept on competing. Following his long string of jujutsu and judo victories, he decided to test his skills in mixed martial arts via the Ultimate Fighting Championship. On February 16, 1996, Moreira fought the 6-foot-8-inch, 360-pound Paul Varelans in the UFC 8 and lost by a narrow decision.

Following that appearance in the UFC, Moreira encountered his first controversy with the Brazilian jujutsu world. At a time when there was an unwritten rule that all black belts were prohibited from teaching jujutsu techniques to non-Brazilian *vale tudo* fighters, Moreira started to teach his good friend, Kimo Leopoldo (who lost to Royce Gracie in UFC 3). The Brazilian jujutsu community was shocked by this breach of protocol and labeled Moreira a traitor.

Eighteen months later, following his first MMA victory over Yuri Vaulin at the UFC 14, Moreira shocked the Brazilian jujutsu community again by revealing that he trained with Marco Ruas to fight the Russian boxer—without the help of the Gracie family or any of the Brazilian jujutsu community. Seeing the good ground technique presented by Ruas, who trained in jujutsu for 15 years, Moreira gave him a Brazilian jujutsu black belt and caused a commotion amongst his fellow Brazilians. These two important decisions helped pave the way for cross-training to take its now-prominent role in fight training.

Today, Moreira is married with four kids and lives in Newport, California. The seventh-*dan* black belt teaches seminars around the globe and conducts private lessons. Considered a *bona fide* authority on jujutsu, Moreira has issued 30 black belts and released a total of 38 instructional tapes that are considered among the best available in the United States.

—Alexandre Lobo and Marcelo Alonso
Subeditor and editor of Tatame magazine (Brazil)

TABLE OF CONTENTS

FOREWORD

When it comes to concrete description, Brazilian *jujutsu* is one of the most elusive subjects in the martial arts. There are no *kata*, no hard and fast forms or styles that can be illustrated step-by-step via static images and text without losing a great deal of subtlety and fluidity.

Yet despite its enigmatic tendencies, Brazilian jujutsu is not a radical science. It follows the path of least resistance, thrives on surprise and reversal and is less interested in power than in technique. Perhaps this is what makes Brazilian jujutsu so popular today. It allows the smaller, wiser man to prevail against a physically imposing opponent. The confidence that such knowledge imparts also goes a long way in winning the mental battle, thus evening otherwise unfair odds.

With that in mind, it is important to underscore that this book is but a fraction of what is possible in the realm of Brazilian jujutsu. It is a compendium of Joe Moreira's understanding of one aspect of the art: the side mount. As such, it would be difficult to rearrange the order of his techniques without disrupting the flow that they describe. Instead, this book offers both a table of contents and a reference guide that identifies these techniques by their finishes. You may read *Brazilian Jujutsu Side-Mount Techniques* from the beginning to appreciate this particular flow, or you may return to it for explanation of some finer points. Either way, you are bound to reach a deeper appreciation and understanding of this art, whether you are a student, a teacher or simply a fan of the sport.

–Edward Pollard, Assistant Editor, Black Belt Communications LLC

THE MOREIRA PERSPECTIVE

BRAZILIAN JUJUTSU COMES TO AMERICA

In 1914 Japanese master jujutsu instructor Mitsuo Maeda, also known as "Count Koma," immigrated to Brazil and, upon his arrival, was helped greatly by a politician named Gastao Gracie. In return for the favors, Maeda taught jujutsu to Gracie's son, Carlos. Before long, Carlos was teaching his brothers-most notably the now-legendary Helio Gracie.

Helio Gracie, being small in stature, began refining the techniques he learned from Carlos for the purpose of giving a smaller person an advantage against someone significantly larger. He discarded techniques that were not realistic in a real fight situation and tweaked others so that leverage and timing became more important than speed and strength.

Thus, the art of Brazilian jujutsu was born.

Rorion Gracie, son of Helio, came to America with the dream of spreading this exciting art throughout the United States. He opened the first stateside Brazilian jujutsu school in the late 1980s.

In the early 1990s, I became one of the first Brazilian black belts to follow Rorion's lead by starting a studio in America. The next step was to establish a way for Brazilian jujutsu students to test their skills. I did this by introducing the first large-scale Brazilian jujutsu tournament in the United States. Four hundred competitors tested their skills in matches against each other. These early competitions were exciting events that usually matched the three strongest teams in the country against each other: Rickson Gracie, the Machado brothers and, of course, my team. The competition was so close and intense that it often came down to the last match or two to determine the winning team. These tournaments inspired more people to take up the study of jujutsu and played an important part in the growth of Brazilian jujutsu in the United States.

Around that time, Rorion Gracie—collaborating with Robert Meyrowitz and Art Davie—conceived and formed the Ultimate Fighting Championship (UFC). This would be the first full-contact fighting competition in the United States, pitting fighters from all forms of martial arts against each other. Gracie, of course, truly believed that Brazilian jujutsu was the most effective of all the martial arts and was determined to prove it. He could have chosen Rickson Gracie, the toughest fighter of the Gracie family, but instead chose the younger and slimmer 175-pound Royce Gracie to represent the family art. Gracie figured that if the unassuming Royce proved victorious against intimidating muscle-bound fighters weighing as much as 100 pounds more, then people would realize that Brazilian jujutsu was the reason. As it turned out, the young fighter shocked the martial arts world by winning 11 straight matches! Brazilian jujutsu was finally a major force on the American martial arts scene.

THE GENTLE ART

Because of the UFC, full-contact fighting has gained worldwide popularity. Today's fighters are much more sophisticated and understand that to be truly effective in the professional fighting arena, cross-training in several different arts is a necessity. They must be as proficient in stand-up fighting as they are in ground fighting. Surely, no professional mixed-martial arts fighter can be successful today without some knowledge of Brazilian jujutsu.

The word jujutsu means "gentle art." By using leverage and redirection of your opponent's movements, less strength and energy are required—thus explaining the description as "soft" or "gentle." It is also referred to as the gentle art because a skilled technician can dominate and control an opponent, then finish the match in a humane fashion if he so chooses.

The theory is that most physical confrontations—some say upward of 95 percent—end up on the ground. Thus, the well-rounded combatant who is proficient in ground fighting will have a clear, definite advantage once the conflict goes to the ground. All of one's stand-up training in the striking arts will instantly "go out the window." One well-known jujutsu family says it like this: "I am like a shark, the ground is my ocean—and most people don't know how to swim."

TEACHING PHILOSOPHY

I was fortunate to be taught and influenced by many great Brazilian jujutsu players. The most influential of these fighters was Reylson Gracie, who was taught by his uncle, Helio Gracie. However, when I ventured out on my own and opened my first school in America, I instituted my own philosophy or teaching style and called it "sequential learning." The idea is to teach a technique and then immediately teach a sequence of techniques related to the first. The sequence of techniques will usually be based on your opponent's response to the initial technique. For example, if you apply a certain type of armbar and your opponent bends his arm one way to thwart the armbar, you employ the appropriate technique in the series for the opponent's countermeasure. If the opponent goes the opposite direction with his arm, you then apply a third option. He may turn his body toward you, so you apply option four. If he turns his body away from you, you may apply option five, etc.

Another example of this sequential style is when your opponent counters your initial technique, you re-counter, he counters that, and so you re-counter with yet another technique. Obviously this can go on endlessly, but the idea is to think ahead and be aware of your opponent's possible next move. Like a chess player, the jujutsu fighter is thinking two, three or four steps ahead of his or her opponent. Consequently, when there are two very skilled opponents, the one who has the best forward thinking will have the best chance of winning the match.

I don't necessarily teach one move and drill it repeatedly. While I do incorporate drilling into practice sessions, I prefer that my students get the most for their money. That's why I teach many techniques per session—usually at least six, but sometimes as many as 15. My goal is to eventually teach my students every technique in my repertoire. Then each student can make up his own mind as to which techniques he wants to make his own and practice them in his own time. I know that no one can perfect every technique, but by making yourself aware of as many options and proven techniques as possible, you stand a better chance of not getting caught by a surprise move.

Different techniques work better for certain body types among individual practitioners, as well as when they face variously sized opponents and their respective fighting styles. Because of this, during private lessons I spend more time teaching my student the moves that make more sense for (or better fit) his size or personal abilities.

There is a rumor in the jujutsu industry that many Brazilian instructors only teach basics and hold back certain techniques so that the Brazilian competitors always have an advantage over their American counterparts, or so that the instructor always maintains an advantage over their students. While this may be true in some cases, or simply a rumor or a misconception, don't count me among the rascals of such a teaching philosophy. In fact, as I said before, I usually show more than most students can possibly absorb in one session. Sometimes I'm even accused of teaching too many moves per class. In my opinion, the student will eventually catch on through a kind of osmosis. That is, if the technique doesn't immediately become part of his repertoire, maybe the third or fourth time around the technique will "click." In some cases it may take a couple of years for the student to grasp the full value of a given technique and add it to his game.

I also teach a style of control before introducing submission. It is important for a student to be able to learn to dominate and control his opponent to achieve good position for submission. If a novice student starts putting submission before control, he has a tendency to bypass much of the process of learning to grapple. The jujutsu community is littered with students who have virtually no expertise in passing the guard because they are more interested in going straight to the more flashy leg-lock submission. For the same reason, I rarely teach leg locks to a beginning student. Why give up good position for a risky submission attempt that will likely land you in a bad position? I want every student to have a good working knowledge of the overall grappling process, as well as a thorough understanding of positional dominance and control. When a student has a good grasp of these skills and knows how to apply them, his options for submitting an opponent will increase dramatically.

In order to dominate from a position, you must learn to apply weight in the right place with maximum force but minimum effort. If applied correctly, you feel significantly heavier than you actually are. You tightly squirm your way into dominant positions like a boa constrictor, never giving your opponent any space to operate and no chance to escape. When he is trapped and unable to move, you inch your way into the submission in a manner where speed is not necessary. That is the Joe Moreira style: complete dominance with submission as the ultimate goal.

The ability to escape bad positions is also high on my priority list. If you are unable to improve your position when trapped, how will you ever obtain the positional dominance necessary to submit your opponent? I teach every possible escape technique from every conceivable position. For example, the transition from escaping a dangerous position is also a good time to spring a surprise submission. This is a fact that many students initially overlook before they come to me.

Relaxation is key, both physically and mentally. You need to sense the movements of your opponent at all times and never panic, no matter how tight the hold. A tense, panicking fighter will not only miss opportunities, but will run out of gas much sooner than he otherwise would have. You will hear this advice a lot in my class: relax, not so much strength, slow down, think. I know how important strength, conditioning and flexibility all are, but they are secondary to technical expertise.

I never want to stop learning. The art is constantly evolving and improving, and for this reason I need to stay open to suggestions and listen to what my students have to say. Even beginners may have something new to offer. I am constantly developing new moves, new sequences and new angles on existing techniques. Jujutsu has taught me about life, and the lessons I've learned from it have helped me to deal with its trials and tribulations. Jujutsu is the true source of all my success.

Technique 1
SHIFTING CONTROL POSITION TO OPPOSITE SIDE

Starting in the standard side mount position, establish a central position over the opponent's chest and make your weight heavy on his chest. Keep your butt low and your lower knee tight to his body. Put both hands over his body with elbows on the ground, pushing tight against his body.

Switch your lower hand (in this case your left) to the near side of his body. Extend your left leg behind you and slide your right leg through toward his legs, landing on your right hip to establish a strong, wide leg base.

Put your left foot back on the ground and slide your right leg back underneath, moving your trunk over his head. Remain in a low position to restrict his ability to maneuver. Maintain control of his right arm as you turn and pin his other arm across his body with your chest.

Once both arms are immobilized, keep your right foot on the ground and swing your left leg underneath to land on your left hip – again establishing a strong, wide leg base. You have now successfully switched control position sides.

Note the wide stance that gives you a good base so the opponent cannot throw him backward with his left arm. You are now in a position to obtain the full-mount position or apply various finishing techniques.

Technique 2

ANOTHER VARIATION OF
SHIFTING CONTROL POSITION TO OPPOSITE SIDE

Starting in the standard side mount position, establish a central position over the opponent's chest. Keep your butt low and your lower knee tight to his body as you push your weight upon his chest. Put both hands over his body with elbows on the ground and tight against his body.

Place your left foot on the ground and slide your right leg through toward his head, landing on your right hip while simultaneously bringing your left arm on the other side of his body and locking his right arm under your left arm. Again it is very important to keep your left foot way back for a wide strong base.

With your weight on your right elbow, put your left knee on the ground above his head. Keep your butt low as you move, bringing his right arm across his body and trapping it under your chest.

Switch your left arm to the other side of his body. Fall back on your left hip, placing your right foot way back toward his legs, and bring your right arm near the side of his body and immobilize his left arm. You are now in a good control position to effect various submissions.

Technique 3

ATTACKING OPPOSITE ARM
WITH KNEE ON BELLY, STRAIGHT-ARM ELBOW LOCK

Where the opponent places his arms in relation to your arm location is key to what technique will be performed. In this case his left arm is on the lower side of your head in relation to his body. From standard side mount position with both arms over, your right arm slides below his left triceps. Place your left hand on the ground against his head.

Push your body up with your left arm and place your right knee on his stomach.

Slide your right wrist tightly up his arm until you reach his elbow. Pinch his wrist between your neck and shoulder. Grab your own hand and pull it toward your body to finish the straight arm elbow lock.

Technique 4
REVERSE AMERICAN LOCK

When attempting the straight arm elbow lock, your opponent frees his hand from between your shoulder and neck, bending it toward his legs. Maintain control of his triceps with your right hand and place your left hand back on the ground temporarily for base.

Place your right hand on your left biceps, grab his wrist with your left hand and turn your body toward his head to apply the lock. *(Note the placement of Joe's thumbs.)*

Technique 5
SPIN TO OPPOSITE SIDE, ARMBAR

When you attempt the previous technique, your opponent grabs his *gi* or belt to prevent it. Hold on to his left triceps with your right hand and pull it toward your body. Place your left hand on the ground for base.

Bring your left foot to the other side of his body as you spin your body around. Grab under his leg to help you spin and to better control him. Keep as low and tight as possible.

Your left foot stays planted on the ground while the right foot goes over his head. Keep your knees together and fall back to the armbar while still holding on to his leg. You can finish it here or let go of the leg and hold his wrist with both hands.

Technique 6
AMERICAN LOCK

Begin in the standard side mount position with both arms over the opponent's body. Your opponent places his left forearm under your neck or face to keep your weight off or prepare for his escape. Note that your opponent has his arm placed on the upper side of your head in relation to his body.

Pull his left elbow in toward you with your right hand. Try to lock his wrist between the side of your face and left shoulder and use your upper-body weight to pressure his arm to the floor.

Your left hand grips his left wrist and holds it tight to the ground. Keep your elbow on the ground and tightly against his head. Slide your right hand under his triceps and grab your own left wrist. Both grips are done without thumbs.

Slide his elbow back toward his legs and lift it up, always keeping his wrist tight to the ground.

Technique 7
STRAIGHT-ARM AMERICAN LOCK

Your opponent straightens his arm to defend the American Lock, so continue to straighten his arm. Push your body forward slightly toward his wrist and lift his elbow again while tightly holding his wrist to the ground.

Technique 8
REVERSE AMERICAN LOCK

Your opponent is able to free his wrist and bends his arm toward his legs. Keep pressure on his arm to keep it away from his body so he can't grab his gi.

Pin his wrist to the ground with your right hand, reach underneath his triceps to grab your planted left arm and lift his elbow off the ground to apply the reverse American lock or shoulder lock.

Technique 9
KIMURA

Plant your left hand under your opponent's neck and cup his left triceps with your right arm.

Quickly bring your left arm on the other side of his face and on the ground for base while lifting his left arm up toward your face.

Bring your knee over his head and plant it on the ground to keep his head from moving. Bring his left elbow tight to your chest and cup his wrist with your left hand while simultaneously grabbing your own left biceps with your right hand. Now lift up your body and turn it toward his head to finish the *kimura*.

If your opponent is able to grab his gi and flatten his body back to the ground to avoid the kimura, bring your left leg back to the other side of his head. Force your elbow against his wrist to keep his arm pinned to the ground.

Reverse your grip on his left wrist, moving it to the top of his wrist and keeping it tight to the ground. Pull your right arm free and plant it on the other side of his body and do a push-up. (not shown)

While continuing to maintain the grip on his wrist, come up on your left foot, pull his elbow up high and force the wrist back to apply the lock.

Technique 11

LEG-OVER-BACK KIMURA

Your opponent tries to come up when you are applying the previous technique.

Let him drive you backward. Fall back and maintain the lock on his left arm.

Re-planting your left foot, swing your right leg over his back so he can't roll out of the position. Apply the lock.

Technique 12

SPIN-TO-OPPOSITE-SIDE ARMBAR

Your left arm is under your opponent's head with the palm of your left hand on the ground.

Hold on to his left triceps with your right hand and pull it toward your body. Place your left hand on the ground on the other side of his head for base.

Keeping as low and tight as possible, spin your body around so your left foot takes the place of your left hand.

Grab under his leg with your left hand to help you spin and to better control him.

Your left foot swings over his body and the other goes over his head. Keep your knees together and fall back to lock the armbar.

Technique 13
SIT-UP TO ELBOW LOCK

Your opponent counters the armbar by turning his thumb toward your head, twisting his body and walking around in the direction of your head, and comes up to his knees (not shown). Hang on to his arm, turn toward his legs, lean on your right side, and place your left foot inside his left thigh.

Place your right palm on the ground and continue to sit up. Keep your foot inside his thigh and straighten your leg to apply downward pressure on his elbow.

KICK OVER TO ARMBAR

Your opponent bends his arm toward his legs to avoid the pressure on his elbow.

Pull his arm toward you.

Fall back sharply, continue pulling his arm toward you and kick him over, forcing him to do a forward roll.

Lay all the way back, making sure your left leg ends up over his body while pulling his arm to your chest.

Now bring the other leg over his head and complete the armbar.

Technique 15

SHIN-BLOCKS-FACE ARMBAR

Opponent shoves your right leg off his head and places the weight of his head on top of that leg to avoid the previous armbar.

Release your left leg from the top of his body and shove your shin against the side of his face to keep him from coming up toward you.

Squeeze your knees together and apply the armbar. Place the right leg back over his head to better control him. (not shown)

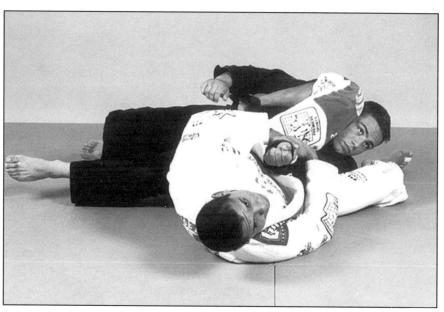

If you are unable to get your shin in front of his face in time to apply the previous lock, block his body with your knee and apply the armbar from there.

Technique 17
ELBOW LOCK FROM TRIANGLE POSITION

In the previous technique, you are unable to stop your opponent with your knee and he attempts to come up to his knees. Swing your left leg over his head and hold on to his arm with both hands.

Shove his left arm to the right side of your body with your left hand and lock your legs above his head as you move off your side and on to your back.

Lock your legs tightly in triangle position. Trap his left arm on the right side of your body by clamping down with your right arm. Hold on to your leg with your right hand, squeeze your knees together and raise your body up to finish the elbow lock.

Technique 18

STRAIGHT-ARM ELBOW LOCK

Begin in basic side mount with your right arm over your opponent's body and left arm under his head. Opponent places his left hand on your right shoulder.

Quickly pull your left arm out and place it on the ground on the far side of his head. Using that left hand for base, shift your weight on to it and swing your left leg around and over his head.

Continue to pull his arm up on your shoulder if it slips down.

Place your left foot on the ground and come up on your right knee. Keep his head immobilized with your legs. Pinch his arm between your shoulder and your neck. Cup your hands together and slide up until you reach the elbow or just under it. Pull toward your body and apply the straight-arm elbow lock.

Technique 19

SIT BACK TO STRAIGHT-ARM ELBOW LOCK

Your opponent attempts to come up on his knees to relieve the pressure on his elbow. Sit back as far as you can from his body, swing your left leg over his head and continue to apply pressure to the elbow.

Squeeze your right knee tight against the opponent's arm.

Technique 20

SEATED ELBOW LOCK TO SHOULDER LOCK

In this case you've made the mistake of sitting back too close to the opponent's body, allowing him to come up and bend his arm to the rear to relieve the pressure against his elbow. Fall back and lean to your left side to free your right foot from the side of his body.

Place your left foot on the ground and pivot your body until your head is positioned toward his legs. Straighten your right leg and use it to drive his shoulder to the ground. At this point his left arm will be trapped between your legs.

Sit up and grab over his body with your left hand to prevent him from rolling out of the hold. Point both feet away from him, adjust your hips away from his body to further break him down and put more pressure on the shoulder.

Lean forward toward his head to finish the shoulder lock.

Technique 21

NECK CRANK FROM SHOULDER LOCK POSITION

Your opponent does not tap from the shoulder lock, so continue to hold the lock on his arm, reach forward and pull up on his head with both hands to apply pressure on the neck.

MAINTAINING THE SHOULDER LOCK

Your opponent comes up to his knees in an attempt to lift you up to relieve the downward pressure on his shoulder.

Adjust your hips away from his body to drive him back down.

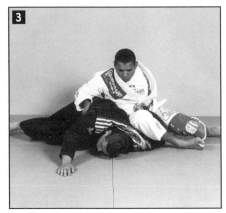

Adjust a little further and begin to lean forward again.

Continue to lean your body forward to finish the shoulder lock.

Technique 23

DOUBLE SHOULDER LOCK

Your opponent places his right hand on the ground as he prepares to lift you up in order to escape the shoulder lock.

Opponent continues to lift up to relieve the downward pressure on his shoulder.

Opponent is able to drive you back. Continue to hold on to his trapped arm with your left hand.

Reach up and grab his other arm or hold on to his upper body with your right hand. Apply downward pressure on his shoulder with your right leg.

Continue to hold on to his arm or body tightly with your right hand. Hook your right foot under your left calf and lock your legs together.

Cinch down your hold on his two trapped arms.

Rock yourself up and drive his left shoulder back to the ground.

Pull back on his right arm to apply the double shoulder lock.

Technique 24

KNEES-ON-FLOOR ELBOW LOCK

Your opponent's left arm is placed on your right shoulder. Trap his left arm with your right hand. Plant your left hand on the floor beside his head.

Putting your weight on your left arm for base, bring your left knee over his head. Pull his arm tight to your chest.

He rolls underneath you to attempt his escape, so bring your head down to the ground while bringing your right knee forward in a crawling motion across his stomach. Keep his arm tight to your chest.

Slide your knee in front of his body. Slide both hands under his elbow and pull up while driving his wrist to the ground with your head and right shoulder.

Technique 25

KNEES-ON-FLOOR ELBOW LOCK TO STRAIGHT-ARM AMERICAN LOCK

Your opponent turns his wrist to avoid the submission. Keep your weight down on him.

Hold his arm tight to your chest with your left arm. Let go with the right, reach forward and grab his wrist while simultaneously grabbing your right wrist with your left. Lift his elbow while tightly holding his wrist to the ground to apply the submission.

Technique 26
REVERSE TRIANGLE TO REVERSE SHOULDER LOCK

Your opponent frees his arm to and bends it downward to avoid the previous submission. *(Note: This technique is to be applied only if his right arm is trapped between your legs.)*

Reach under his left arm with your left arm and grab your own gi lapel. Reach back and grab his trapped right arm with your right hand.

Lean forward and place your left leg over his head and then under his neck. Triangle your other leg by placing your left foot on top of your right calf in order to lock his head.

Fall over to your left side, keeping your legs locked tight.

Begin pushing his trapped right wrist with your right hand away. Continue pushing until you apply the shoulder lock.

Technique 27
REVERSE TRIANGLE TO WRIST LOCK

Your opponent is aware of your previous technique and hides his right arm low enough so that you are unable to reach it with your right hand.

View from opposite side

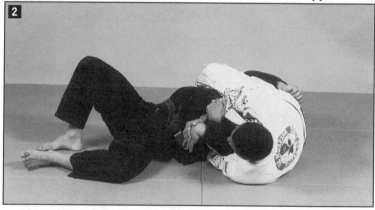

So now attack his other arm. The left arm that is trapping his left arm reaches through and grabs your right wrist. Grab his left hand with your right hand and pull it toward you while you lock his elbow against your chest to apply the wrist lock.

REVERSE TRIANGLE TO STRAIGHT-ARM ELBOW LOCK

Opponent defends the previous wrist lock by straightening his arm.

Grab his left arm, pull it under your head and lock it there.
Continue to hold tightly to his arm with your other arm.

Hug his arm tightly to your body with both arms and
straighten your body to apply the elbow lock.

Technique 29

STEP OVER/LEAN BACK ELBOW LOCK

You are in standard side mount control position. Your opponent attempts to push your hip away to make space for his escape. Reach down and grab his right elbow that is pushing against your hip with your left hand.

Go up on your toes and change your base by shooting your right leg under your left and scissor toward his head. Pull up on his right arm and trap it beneath your underarm, all the while maintaining a tight grip on his other shoulder with your other arm.

Step over his head with your left foot. Grab your leg with your left hand, keeping his arm tightly locked under your arm, and lean back with your upper torso to apply the elbow lock.

STEP OVER/LEAN BACK ELBOW LOCK VARIATION

From the previous position, lean forward and plant your knee on the ground and immobilize your opponent's head. Grab your upper thigh with your left hand and lean slightly back with your upper torso while keeping your butt down to apply the elbow lock.

Technique 31
FALL BACK TO ARMBAR

While attempting the previous technique, your opponent is able to free his arm to prevent the submission.

Keep his right arm trapped, lift up your upper torso, and place your right foot on the ground.

Fall back to armbar position shown previously, pulling both of his arms if possible.

Fall back, squeeze your knees together, raise your hips while holding his right wrist in thumb-up position with both hands, and complete the armbar.

From *kesa gatame* (basic pinning technique), your opponent grabs your near collar with his left hand.

He turns toward you and pushes you away. Keep your right arm over his left as he pushes.

Lock his left arm with your right and grab it with your left. Using his momentum, turn away from him and pull his arm across.

Continue to pull his arm across, turning him on his side. Your right arm is leveraged down on top of his left arm. Place your left hand under his left wrist and clasp your hands to begin tightening the lock.

Apply all your body weight down on his upper arm and pull up on his wrist to finish the lock.

Technique 33
PULL-ACROSS ELBOW LOCK FAILS TO AMERICAN LOCK

Your opponent manages to free his locked arm.

As he attempts to pull his arm back, switch your grip by bringing your left hand to the top of his wrist and gripping your own wrist. Begin to turn toward him, keeping your body tight against his to prevent him from wriggling free or slipping out while you make the transition.

Continue to turn to your knees to standard side-mount position while driving his wrist to the ground. Finish with the American Lock previously shown.

Technique 34

LEG-OVER-HEAD CHOKE

Start again from the kesa gatame control position …

… lean forward and reach deep into his right lapel behind his ear.

Step over his head with your left foot and pull up on his lapel to apply the choke.

Technique 35
KNEE-ON-STOMACH FALL TO UNDERARM ARMBAR

Opponent attempts to lift you up. Place both hands on the floor.

Allow opponent to lift you up. Place your right knee in his stomach.

Bring your left foot forward and lift his right arm by grabbing at the triceps just below the elbow with your left hand.

Throw your hips forward and lift your head up.

Step over his head with your left leg and fall back while holding on to both arms if possible.

Get your left foot positioned tight against his body and lean back, raising your hips and squeezing your knees together to apply the arm lock under your arm.

Technique 36

SPIN TO KNEE BAR ON FAR LEG

Prepare to move to the knee-on-stomach position.

As you come up to enter the knee, your opponent pushes you up with his arms and blocks you with his knee that is nearest to you.

Reach under and grab his far leg with your right arm.

Bring your left knee across his body and spin toward his legs, hugging his leg tight to your body using both arms.

Fall to the opposite side of his body, swing your right leg over his leg and hug it tight to your body as you squeeze your knees together. Then thrust your hips forward as you lean your upper body back to apply the knee bar.

You can also reach in front of his leg with your right arm while you hold his leg with your left arm and lock his leg under your arm. Hug his leg to your body while grabbing your right thigh for a more powerful finish.

Technique 37
SPIN TO KNEE BAR ON NEAR LEG

As you come up to enter the knee, your opponent pushes you up with his arms and blocks you with his knee that is nearest to you.

Reach under and grab the blocking leg with your right arm. Bring your left knee across his body and spin toward his legs.

Hugging his leg tight to your body with both arms, fall to the opposite side of his body. Swing your right leg over his hugged leg and pull it tight to your body as you squeeze your knees together. Thrust your hips forward as you lean your upper body back to apply the knee bar.

WRIST LOCK AGAINST CHEST

Your opponent hides his arms under your body while you have both arms over his body.

Pull his left elbow to the side of his body with both hands, keeping your chest weight pressing down.

Place your right hand on his biceps, bring your body forward and push his elbow toward your body.

Push his arm to the ground with your right hand and your left hand pulls his elbow toward you.

Now pull his elbow toward your body with both hands while applying downward pressure with your chest, causing his wrist to bend to complete the wrist lock.

Technique 39
HAND-OVER-ARM NECK CRUNCH

Begin in standard side mount with your left arm under his neck. Make sure you get his right arm trapped between your left arm and your left leg. Drive your left knee forward to tighten the hold.

Push his left elbow up toward his head with your right hand. Pick up on his head with your left arm. Reach over his left arm and pull it back with your left hand.

Move your legs around toward his head so you can drive his head toward his legs with your left upper arm while continuing to pull back on his left arm with your hand. Keep your body weight low and tight as you drive your torso down his body. *(Always be careful in practice! This is a dangerous technique and could result in a broken neck).*

Technique 40
LEG-OVER-ARM NECK CRUNCH

If your opponent does not submit to the previous technique, place your left foot over his left arm and drop your knee to the floor. Once again, drive his neck forward while pulling back on his arm with your leg.

Technique 41
LEG-OVER-ARM NECK CRUNCH PULLING HEAD

If he still does not submit, lock your hands together and pull up on his head with both arms.

Technique 42

LEG-OVER-ARM NECK CRUNCH TO ARMBAR

If the previous techniques don't work or you simply want to go straight to this one, lean forward and place your left hand on the ground for base. Lift your right knee up and place your foot on the floor next to your opponent's body. Reach down and grab his right leg behind the knee with your right hand and pull it toward you.

Lean your body toward his legs so you can free up the left leg to go over his head. Grab under his right arm with your left arm.

Fall back and continue swinging your left leg over his head to complete the armbar. *(Note: You may choose to keep his right arm trapped under your left underarm when you fall back to the armbar. If you do, fall back slowly in practice since this can badly injure your training partner).*

Technique 43

LEG-OVER-ARM NECK CRUNCH TO COLLAR CHOKE

Begin in standard side mount with your left arm under your opponent's neck. Make sure you get his right arm trapped between your left arm and your left leg. Drive your left knee forward to tighten the hold.

Push his left elbow up toward his head with your right hand. Push up on his head with your left arm. Reach over his left arm and pull it back with your left hand.

Bring your left foot over his left arm and plant it on the ground while planting your right hand on the ground in front of his body to maintain a good base.

Grab his top collar with your right hand and feed it to your left hand. Pull back with your left hand while pulling his other collar away and down with your right hand to apply the collar choke.

Technique 44

LEG-OVER-ARM NECK CRUNCH TO COLLAR CHOKE WITH TRIANGLE AND ARMBAR

If you are having trouble submitting your opponent with the previous technique, let go with your right hand, maintain your left hand grip and fall back while swinging your right leg over his body.

Triangle your legs, trap his right arm under your left arm and lean back for the underarm arm lock combined with a triangle choke.

Technique 45

NECK CRANK FROM SIDE MOUNT

Your opponent's left arm is under your neck and his hand is placed on your left shoulder.

Grab under his left elbow, lifting your head and chest up slightly. Use your right hand to push his elbow across toward your right shoulder.

Drop your upper-torso weight and lower your head behind his triceps to lock his arm against his head.

Drop your head low and tight behind his left triceps to prevent him from freeing his arm. Squeeze your arms together and drive your weight down to apply the neck crank.

Technique 46

NECK CRANK FROM MOUNT

From the previous technique, continue to tighten your grip and prepare to mount.

Take the mount position. Place your left hand on your right biceps, drive your weight forward and squeeze his neck for the submission.
(Note: For an even stronger submission, you can hop off the mount to his left side and continue the neck crank.)

PUSH ELBOW/SHOULDER LOCK FROM HEAD LOCK POSITION

Your opponent reaches his left hand under your right arm.

Turn toward his head and place your left foot on the ground for balance. Release your left arm from under his head and replace it with your right.

Bring your right leg underneath your left and lay on your right hip while pulling up on his right arm with your left. Establish a wide base with your legs.

Allow your opponent to pull his trapped arm out slightly but lock his wrist tightly under your left arm.

Place your left hand on the inside of his right elbow and push it away from your body to apply the shoulder lock.

Technique 48
WRIST LOCK FROM HEAD LOCK POSITION

As your opponent attempts to free his right hand from beneath your left underarm, grab outside his elbow and pull toward your chest as you lean forward to trap his bent wrist against your chest or shoulder.

Technique 49

BENT-ARM AMERICAN LOCK WITH FRONT LEG

You are holding your opponent in the head lock position.
Grab his right wrist with your left hand.

Shove his wrist beneath your right shin.

Hold his wrist until you can triangle your legs. Pull up on his
head and lean your body forward to apply the submission.

Technique 50

STRAIGHT-ARM ELBOW LOCK WITH REAR LEG

Your opponent tries to straighten his right arm to avoid the submission from the previous technique. Continue to hold onto his wrist as he straightens his arm.

Force his right wrist under your left leg.

Hook his arm under your left leg as your left hand releases his wrist.

Lean heavily on his chest, lift your right knee up as you force your left leg back and down on his arm to apply the submission.

PRETZEL CHOKE FROM HEAD LOCK POSITION

Your opponent bends his arm back to avoid the previous technique, so continue to trap his right arm with your left leg and continue to hold your right leg with your right hand to tightly secure his head. Reach across his neck with your left hand, grab your right biceps, and drive your left wrist/forearm forward and down against his neck.

Swing your right leg back under your left and shift onto your knees, keeping your weight down.

Drive your forearm and your upper-body weight down to apply the choke.

Technique 52

BASEBALL BAT CHOKE

Your left arm is under your opponent's head and your right arm is on the other side of his body, below his arm.

Reach deep under his neck with your left hand and grab his left collar with your four fingers on the outside.

Pull your right hand up and grab his left collar with four fingers inside.

Lift your body up, bring your right knee up against his right arm on the ground, spreading your legs wide for a good base. Push your right forearm down into his neck while lifting up and straightening your left arm, bringing your elbows together to apply the choke.

Your left arm is under your opponent's head and your right arm is on the other side of his body, below his arm. Reach deep under his neck with your left hand and grab his left collar with your four fingers on the outside.

Pull your right hand up, lift your body and grab his right collar deep with four fingers inside.

Lift his head, swinging your left elbow over and around it to the opposite side.

Drop your left forearm across his neck and press your weight to apply the choke.

Technique 54

CROSS CHOKE BLOCKING WITH KNEE

Opponent attempts to snake his hips away from you to avoid the pressure of the choke.

Place your right knee against his hip to anchor him and continue to apply the choke.

ROLL-TO-THE-MOUNT CROSS CHOKE

Your opponent blocks the choke from the previous technique by snaking his hip in toward you.

Begin to slide your right knee over his body to take the mount while maintaining the choke hold and bring your upper body down to finish the choke.

Your opponent begins to roll you, so hang on to the choke.

Continue to hold on to the choke as you roll to the guard position.

Twist your wrists in toward one another and pull him close to your chest to finish the choke.

Technique 56

TRAP WRIST TO WRIST LOCK

Your right arm is positioned across your opponent's upper body and your left arm is under his head. His left arm is attempting to push away your face.

Shove his elbow with your right hand so his left arm is across his face. Lock the arm there with your chin and your upper-body weight.

Grab his wrist with your left hand, reach your right arm below his head and feed his wrist to that hand.

Let go of his wrist and trap it against the ground. Push your weight down on his trapped arm as you hold on to his head with your left hand to apply the wrist lock.

TRAP WRIST TO FOREARM CHOKE

Start with the first three moves of the previous technique.

Continue to hold your opponent's wrist. Reach your left hand behind his trapped arm and across his neck. Pull on his wrist and straighten your other arm to apply the choke.

Technique 58

TRAP WRIST FAILS TO AMERICAN LOCK

Your opponent is able to free his trapped wrist.

As he frees his left hand, stay low and follow his arm across his body with your head against his freed arm.

Push his wrist against the ground with your left hand.

Reach your right hand beneath his left arm and grab your own left wrist.

Slide his arm back and lift his elbow to apply the American lock.

COUNTER AMERICAN LOCK DEFENSE WITH SIT-UP ARM LOCK

Your opponent attempts to free his arm from the American lock by snaking his hips to the right and pushing against your left underarm with his right hand.

Keep his wrist trapped against the ground for base and bring your left foot forward.

Continue to bring your left foot forward, keeping his right arm trapped with your body.

Step your left foot forward over his head and onto the ground. Grab the outside of your left knee with your left hand, lift your body and pull back on his straightened arm to apply the upright arm lock.

Technique 60
FALL TO UNDERARM ARMBAR

Your opponent is able to bend his arm to prevent the previous technique's arm lock.

Place your right foot on the ground with your knee up in front of his body and fall back, keeping his arm trapped under your arm.

Fall back while holding his right leg with your right hand to prevent him from rolling over the top to escape. Finish the underarm armbar.

Technique 61

TRAP SHOULDER, FOREARM CHOKE

Start from side-control position with both arms over your opponent's body. Grab his left shoulder and secure his arm with your right hand. Keep your left elbow tight against his head to prevent him from moving and trying to escape. Bring your left knee up tight to trap his right arm.

Release his left shoulder and bring your right hand to the other side of his body to trap his right shoulder.

Keep his right arm trapped and begin to bring your left forearm across his neck.

Grab his left shoulder with your left hand and apply downward pressure against his neck with your forearm. Straighten your legs and drop all your body weight down on his neck to apply the choke.

Technique 62
TRAP SHOULDER, FOREARM CHOKE TO ARMBAR

Begin to apply the previous technique.

As you attempt to bring your left forearm down against your opponent's neck, he defends by pushing you away with his right arm. Pull up on his right triceps with your right hand.

Place your left hand on the ground for base. Lean forward and bring your left knee over his face and on the ground, securely trapping his arm with your body.

Bring your left arm under his right arm and hug it to your body.

Grab under his right leg with your right arm and begin to sit.

Fall back to the ground, let go of his leg, and use both arms to secure his and complete the armbar.

Technique 63
STRAIGHT-ARM ELBOW LOCK FROM HEAD MOUNT

From the head mount or north/south position, your opponent exposes his left arm in front of your left arm.

Force his left arm up by pulling your arm toward your body as you raise your upper torso.

Force your left arm across his chest to your right side as far as possible. Place your right hand on top of your left, causing your hold on his arm to tighten and straighten even more. Force your head to the left and pull his triceps just below the elbow toward your chest to apply the submission.

Technique 64
STRAIGHT-ARM ELBOW LOCK TO KIMURA

While attempting the previous technique, your opponent is able to free his left arm and pull it down below your head. Follow his arm down with your upper torso and block his arm with your head from reaching across and grabbing his belt or gi.

Reach across with your right hand and grab his left wrist.

Grab your own right wrist with your left hand to apply a figure-four type lock on his arm.

Lift his arm up off the ground, pulling his elbow up tight to your chest. Step your left foot on the ground over his head, turn your body toward his head and drive his wrist toward it to apply the submission.

Technique 65
STRAIGHT-ARM ELBOW LOCK TO FALL-BACK ARMBAR

During your attempt of the straight-arm elbow lock shown previously, your opponent is able to free his left arm and pull it down below your head to reach across his body and grab his belt or gi.

Continue holding his left arm with your left arm and place your right hand on the ground for base.

Raise your upper torso, keeping his elbow tight to your chest.

Step over his head with your right leg and place your foot flat on the ground.

Bring your left knee up against his body and begin to position yourself perpendicular to his body. Hold on to your opposite arm with your right hand in order to help bring the opponent's body with you.

Begin to fall back.

Begin to slide your left arm closer to his wrist as you fall back farther.

Fall back all the way to the ground and apply the armbar previously shown.

Technique 66

FOUR-FINGERS-IN/FOUR-FINGERS-OUT FOREARM CHOKE FROM HEAD MOUNT

From the head mount (or north/south position), enter the four fingers of your right hand inside your opponent's right collar.

Sink your hand in deep and put your weight on your fist.

Now enter the thumb of your left hand into his left collar with your four fingers outside of his collar.

Move your body toward the hand that has the four fingers inside (in this case it is the right hand) and bring your knee to that side of his head. Lift your elbow on your left side.

Bring your left arm up and over his head and drive your forearm into his neck.

Sink all your weight onto your forearm to finish the choke.

Technique 67

PRETZEL CHOKE FROM HEAD MOUNT

Your opponent's arms are above your shoulders. Keep your upper-body weight heavy on his.

Reach your left arm under his neck and push his head deeper into your armpit with your right hand.

Slide your right forearm over his neck and place your hand on his chest. Grab your right biceps with your left hand. Lift his head slightly and now drop all your chest weight on to your forearm to finish the choke.

Technique 68

SHOULDER LOCK WITH KNEE FROM HEAD MOUNT

Your opponent has his hands locked around your back below your arms.

Place your hands on the ground for base.

Lift your body to break his locked hands. Place your left foot on the ground and lift your knee to parallel the ascent of your left elbow.

Keep his left arm pinned tightly between your left arm and body. Pinch your knee in toward his body to apply the submission.

Technique 69

AMERICAN LOCK FROM FAILED SHOULDER LOCK

Your opponent bends his arm back to avoid the previous submission. Grab his wrist with your left hand.

Lower your upper torso and reach under his left triceps with your right hand and grab your own left wrist.

Push his wrist to the ground.

Move your knees to his right side. Pull his elbow back and lift his upper left arm to apply the submission.

Use your left knee to pin his head to prevent the escape.

WRIST LOCK FROM FAILED SHOULDER LOCK

Your opponent has his hands locked around your back below your arms.

Place your hands on the ground for base and lift your body to break his locked hands. Place your left foot on the ground and lift your knee to attempt the shoulder lock.

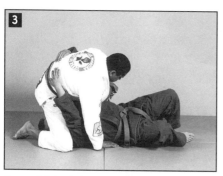

To avoid the lock, your opponent drops his left arm toward his body and grabs his own belt.

Trap his hand with your right hand and begin to slide your left hand below his forearm.

Slide your left hand down toward his wrist and grab your right wrist.

Pull his hand toward you while keeping your chest behind his elbow and apply the wrist lock.

Technique 71

WRIST LOCK BACK TO KIMURA

You were able to break yor opponent's hand free, but unable to finish the wrist lock. Hold his arm tight to your chest and quickly lift your upper body. Keep his wrist high and turn your body to the left.

You can bring your knee over his right arm to stabilize his movement while you apply the kimura.

Technique 72
TRAP SHOULDER FOREARM CHOKE

Both arms are over your opponent's body. He has his right arm on the right side of your body.

Reach under his right arm with your right hand and place four fingers inside his collar. Grab his shoulder with your left hand.

Slide your left forearm tight across his neck.

Straighten your legs to apply all your upper body weight onto your elbow to finish the choke.

Technique 73

FALL BACK TO REVERSE SHOULDER LOCK

Your arms are in front of your opponent's in the north/south position.

Lock his left arm under yours and hold on to his elbow. Move your legs slightly to the left, so you can bring your right hand over the top of his right arm and place it on the floor above his right shoulder.

Continue to move to your left, keeping his left arm trapped. Get up on your toes.

Put your left foot on the ground and scissor your right leg underneath. Keep your weight on his chest at this time.

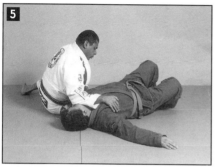

Place your right hand on his upper chest to keep him from rolling toward you. Pull up on his left elbow and begin to sit back.

Continue to sit back.

Fall back and bring your right leg over his body. Lift your hips and apply the shoulder lock.

Technique 74
REVERSE SHOULDER LOCK WITH BOTH LEGS OVER

Your opponent slides his hips toward you and looks away to avoid the pressure on his shoulder from the previous technique.

Swing your second leg over his body and move perpindicular to his body.

Lift your hips to continue the pressure for the submission.

SPIN TO KNEE BAR

Both arms are over your opponent's body. His left knee is up to prevent you from taking the mount position.

Place your left foot on the ground and raise your knee. Bring your left hand to the other side of his body.

Swing your right leg under your left and hug his left knee to your body,

Bring your right knee up inside his trapped leg and begin to fall back.

Fall back and pull his leg toward you.

Squeeze your knees together, hug his leg tight to your chest and lift your hips to finish the knee bar.

Technique 76

KNEE POPPER

Both arms are over your opponent.

He begins to turn toward you to get a better position to escape.

Reach over with your left arm and grab under his right ankle.

Pull his ankle up toward his upper body and grab it with your other hand.

Lock your hands and pull up and in to his body.
(Note: Be extremely careful when practicing this move. This is very dangerous and can easily damage your partner's knee.)

Technique 77
KNEE BAR FROM HALF MOUNT

You are controlling your opponent in the side mount position with your left arm on the near side of his neck and your right arm on the other side of his body.

Opponent begins to push on your hip to begin his escape.

Opponent is able to turn onto his right hip and tries to trap your left leg.

Opponent successfully traps your left leg and places you in his half-guard.

Push yourself down his body while your arms stay tight on each side of his body for control.

Now trap his leg by triangling it with your left foot over the top of your right calf.

Hold his body tightly, push down with your pelvis, and up with your legs to apply the knee bar.

Technique 78
KNEE BAR FROM SIDE

Your opponent attempts to turn onto his left hip in order to relieve the pressure on his knee.

Follow his movement and turn on to your left hip, reach your right arm between his legs and control his right leg while keeping his leg tightly locked.

Bring your right leg back to re-apply the pressure for the knee bar.

Your opponent now rolls you all the way over to again avoid the pressure on his knee.

Slide your body down and grab his leg tightly with both arms. Drive your pelvis up and his lower leg down to again re-apply the pressure for the knee bar.

Technique 80
TOE HOLD FROM TRAPPED LEG

You are controlling your opponent in typical side-mount position with both arms over his body.

Your opponent unwisely traps your left leg with his left leg.

Lift your body and place your left foot on the ground, trapping his left leg between your left arm and left leg.

Turn toward his leg, reach up and place your left hand on top of his left foot while keeping his leg trapped with your right arm.

Reach under his leg and grab your left wrist.

Keeping his leg trapped between your upper body and upper thigh, apply downward pressure at the base of his toes to finish the toe hold.

Technique 81

TOE HOLD TO KNEE BAR

You are controlling your opponent in typical side-mount position with both arms over his body and your opponent unwisely traps your left leg with his left leg.

Lift your body and place your left foot on the ground, trapping his left leg between your left arm and left leg.

Turn toward his leg, reach up and place your left hand on top of his left foot while keeping his leg trapped with your right arm. Reach under his leg and grab your left wrist.

Keep his leg trapped between your upper body and upper thigh and apply downward pressure at the base of his toes to attempt finishing the toe hold.

Your opponent drives his foot to the ground to prevent the toe hold.

Slide your right knee over his stomach and in between his legs.

Roll to your right while maintaining the toe-hold position.

Squeeze your knees together and you now have the option of applying the toe hold or the knee bar.

Technique 82

CROSS-FACE NECK CRANK

Your opponent attempts to escape side control by turning toward you.

He now turns to his knees to escape the side control. Drive your right knee in toward his body and reach across his face with your left hand and grab his right triceps.

Bring your left foot out for a wide base. Keep your left wrist and forearm against the side of his face and grab your left hand with your right hand.

Keep your upper-body weight tight against his upper body.

Bring your right foot forward and pull up on his head/neck to apply the neck crank.

Technique 83
CROSS-FACE LION KILL

Your opponent leaves his neck exposed, so move your body more forward.

Reach deep across his neck and attempt to get the crook of your elbow lined up with the center of his neck. Grab your other biceps.

Pull up with your left arm, reach up behind his neck with your right hand, and squeeze your elbows together to apply the lion-kill choke.

Technique 84

SIT-FORWARD COLLAR CHOKE

Reach under with your left hand and grab your opponent's right gi collar.

Grab his right wrist with your right hand for better control.

Keep your chest tight to his back and step your left foot forward.

Slide your right leg under your left.

Sit your weight on his left shoulder and pull up with your left hand to apply the choke.

Technique 85
HAND-BEHIND-HEAD CHOKE

Your opponent turns his head away to prevent the previous choke.

Deepen your grip and go to your knees.

Reach under his right arm with yours and turn him toward you.

Reach behind his neck and grab your own triceps.

You may be able to finish the choke at this point.

Technique 86

ROLL TO HAND-BEHIND-HEAD CHOKE FROM HIS BACK

Roll backward while maintaining the previous choke.

Slide your left foot under your opponent's body to get the hooks for better control. In case you are unable to get the choke, you will at least have his back. Straighten your left arm and apply the choke.

Technique 87

HAND-BEHIND-HEAD CHOKE FROM HIS BACK TO THE ARMBAR

Abandon the choke and pull on your opponent's right arm with your right arm.

Push his face away with your left hand and begin to position your body perpendicular to his.

Bring your right leg across his body and pull your left leg from beneath his body.

Bring your left leg over his head, grab his wrist with both arms, and fall back to the armbar previously shown.

Technique 88
CLOCK CHOKE WITH BODY WEIGHT

Your opponent has escaped the side control by turning to his knees. He blocks you from coming forward to apply the sit forward collar choke with his left arm.

Grab his other collar with your right hand.

Drop your left knee and your upper-body weight.

Drop your weight forward and pull on both collars to finish the choke.

Technique 89
CRUCIFIX CHOKE

Your opponent has again turned to his knees, escaping the side mount. Bring your right knee into his body. Reach through with your right hand behind his right arm and grab his wrist. Grab his right collar with your left hand with four fingers out.

Bring your left leg forward in front of his left arm.

Drive your left leg under his arm and begin to roll forward.

Turn your head to the inside as you roll forward over your right shoulder.

As you roll over, your opponent will end up on his back

(continued on next page)

Technique 89 (continued)
CRUCIFIX CHOKE

Triangle your legs to lock his left arm and pull your opponent on top of you.

Pull on his collar as you straighten your left arm. Pull his right arm back and away so he can't defend the choke by jerking his collar out of your grip.

Technique 90
CRUCIFIX TO SHOULDER LOCK

If the choke is unsuccessful, you can pull back on his arm with your right arm.

Completely straighten his trapped arm and raise your hips to apply the shoulder lock.

For some reason the shoulder lock was unsuccessful, but you continue to tightly hold on to your opponent's arm.

Bring your left leg across his body as you move your upper body toward your left.

Hook your right leg over your left ankle.

Let go of his arm and use that hand to help you to sit up.

Lift your body off the ground and lean forward to apply the triangle choke. You can grab his gi or belt and pull with your right hand to help you lean forward.

Technique 92
STRAIGHT-ARM LOCK WITH LEGS

Your opponent has again turned to his knees, escaping the side mount. Bring your right knee into his body. Reach through with your left hand behind his right arm and grab his wrist. Your opponent has also made the mistake of exposing his left arm. Get your left leg under his left arm.

Hook your left foot over your right ankle to trap his left arm and begin to lean your body weight forward.

Stretch your body out, lift your legs and drop your hips to apply the arm lock.

Technique 93
BENT-BACK ARM LOCK WITH LEGS

To avoid the pressure of the previous submission attempt, your opponent bends his arm backward.

Uncross your feet but keep his arm trapped between your legs. Pull your right arm out and use your left hand as a base.

Turn your body toward his legs and grab under his left ankle with your right hand.

Fall back toward your left hip and lift your right leg up high and back to apply the arm lock.

Technique 94
BENT-FORWARD ARM LOCK WITH LEGS

To avoid the pressure of the previous submission attempt, your opponent bends his arm forward.

Reach in and trap his right wrist with your left hand. Look forward and keep your upper-body weight heavy on your opponent.

Sit back on your right hip. Pull your leg up and back to apply the arm lock.

BENT-FORWARD ARM LOCK WITH LEGS USING CROSS-FACE

Your opponent begins to turn his body toward you to attempt escape or relieve pressure on his arm. Drive your left arm across his face and lock your hands to apply neck pressure combined with the arm lock.

Technique 96
ROLL TO COLLAR CHOKE

In an attempt to free his arm by driving you back, your opponent lifts his head. Reach over his head with your left hand and grab his left collar.

Begin to reach under his left arm with your right arm.

Stick your head under his body, look forward and reach deep behind his neck with your left hand.

Tuck your head under and roll while holding his left arm tightly.

As you roll through, the momentum will carry his body over yours.

As he rolls over your body, be sure to hold on tightly to his left arm.

Snake your hips back to be more perpendicular to his body.

Swing your left leg under your right until you are flat on your stomach.

Continue to work your body toward perpendicular and cinch in the choke. (You can also come up to your knees for better leverage.)

Technique 97
TURN AND SPIN TO FALL-BACK ARMBAR

Your opponent is again in the turtle position. Come up to your feet with your upper-body weight on his back.

Place your left hand on his neck as your right hand grips his belt.

Press your weight up and straighten your arms, maintaining strong pressure against him to lock him in place.

Step your left foot forward and press your left leg against his body. Step your right foot back.

Swing your right foot in front of his left arm until you are perpendicular to his body.

Reach down and grab his left arm with both your arms.

If he ducks his right shoulder toward the ground to defend, sit down on his body and hug his arm to your chest.

Fall back and finish with the armbar previously shown.

Technique 98

KICK OVER TO ARMBAR FROM TURTLE POSITION

Your opponent is again in the turtle position. Come up to your feet with your upper-body weight on his back.

Press your weight up and straighten your arms, maintaining strong pressure against him to keep him from moving.

Place your left hand on his neck and your right hand grips his belt.

Step your left foot forward up against his body and step your right foot back.

Still holding your oppnent in place, swing your left foot behind his left arm ...

... and begin turning ...

... so you can reach down and grab his left arm with both of your arms. In this case, your opponent does not duck his right shoulder as in the previous technique, but remains up.

This time, hold on to his arm with your right arm only and let go with your left arm. Turn toward his legs, grab his belt with your left hand, and hook your left foot under his left leg.

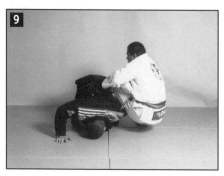

Now sit back toward his head.

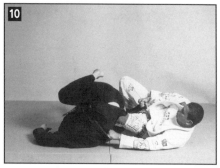

Continue holding his belt, fall back toward his head, and whip him over with your left leg.

Your opponent will be forced to roll over backward. As he rolls over, swing your left leg across his body, and your right leg over his face and apply the armbar.

Technique 99
INNER-LEG COLLAR CHOKE FROM TURTLE POSITION

Your opponent is in the turtle position. Your right arm goes around his body and secures his right wrist. Place your left foot forward and on the ground. Reach under his neck with your left hand and grab his right collar.

Lean your body forward and begin to bring your left leg over his head.

Bring your leg over his head and place your foot on the ground for base.

Pull your calf back against his face.

Press your inner knee against his head and point it under his shoulder while pulling up on the collar to apply the choke.

Technique 100
DOUBLE SHOULDER LOCK FROM TURTLE POSITION

Your opponent is again in the turtle position. Keep you weight across his back to hold him in position.

Base your weight on your hands.

Lift your left leg in front of his left arm and hook under it.

Bring your left leg back and trap his arm by triangling your legs.

(continued on next page)

Technique 100 (continued)
DOUBLE SHOULDER LOCK FROM TURTLE POSITION

Base up on your right hand, and reach under his right arm with your left.

Now reach your left arm behind his head.

Get your left hand down under his head to pull his arm back toward your legs.

Continue pulling his arm back and drop your weight to apply the double shoulder lock.

Technique 101
DOUBLE SHOULDER LOCK FAILS TO COLLAR CHOKE

Your opponent bends his arm back to take the pressure off of his shoulder.

Grab his right collar with your right hand.

Feed the collar to your left hand behind his head.

Slide your right hand across his face and grab your left forearm. Straighten your arms to apply the choke.

Technique 102

COLLAR CHOKE FAILS TO UNDERARM ARM LOCK

Slide your left arm up your opponent's right arm, keeping his arm tightly trapped underneath it.

Place your right hand inside his shoulder, straighten your body and come up to your knees.

Lift your right knee up against his body while keeping everything tight.

Now lift your left leg in preparation to swing it over his head.

Lean slightly to your right in order to take some weight off your left leg, making it easier to swing the leg over his head.

Fall back while still tightly trapping his right arm under your left arm.

Your opponent is in a defensive turtle position. Keep your weight on his body. Reach under his neck with your left hand and grab his right collar with four fingers out and your thumb inside.

Swing your right leg over his body, using your right hand for support.

Maintain a tight grip on his collar.

Shoot your right knee under his body, between his leg and arm.

Shove your right knee all the way under his body. Pull back forcefully on his collar while placing your right arm behind his head to apply additional leverage to finish the choke.

Technique 104

FROM COLLAR CHOKE TO ARM LOCK

If for some reason you are unable to finish the collar choke, note that your opponent's right arm is also vulnerable to attack.

Slide your right hand up your left arm in order to straighten his right arm.

Swing your leg over his head and you continue to straighten your body.

Bring your left leg under his head, squeeze your knees together, hug his arm to your body and arch your body back while thrusting your hips forward to complete the arm lock.

WRIST LOCK TO BREAK THE INSIDE HAND GRIP

In a situation where your opponent grabs his own wrist with the hand of the arm that you are attacking, hold his left elbow against your body with your right arm and use your left hand to cup his hand that is gripping his wrist.

Now slide your right hand down his arm and grab his right hand.

Lift up his arms and lean back to weaken his grip.

Pull his wrist toward you and twist it toward your legs.

Hug his arm with both hands high on his wrist and begin to fall back ...

... finish the armbar.

Technique 106
WRIST LOCK TO BREAK THE OUTSIDE HAND GRIP

Joe lays back so you can see how his opponent might grip his own wrist to defend against an armbar. In this case he grabs his own wrist on his left arm (which is being attacked) with his free arm.

Reach under his left arm with your right arm. Grab your own left forearm. Grab the top of his left hand with your left hand.

Be sure to keep his elbow tight against your chest. Twist his wrist back toward you and toward his legs.

Lean your weight toward his head to finally break his grip.

Once his grip is broken, fall straight back and hug his arm to your body with both arms.

Finish the armbar as shown previously.

Technique 107

WRIST LOCK TO BREAK THE GI GRIP

Your opponent is attempting to prevent the armbar by gripping his own gi with his left arm. Secure his left arm tight against your chest with your right arm. Grip your own gi to assist this action.

Bring your left arm below your right and under his left arm in order to switch grips from right arm to left.

Pull your right arm loose and cup his left hand. Slide your left wrist down close to his and grab your own right wrist.

Keeping his elbow tight against your chest, pull his hand toward you in order to apply pressure by bending his wrist.

At this point, he may submit from the wrist lock itself. If not, you will at least have succeeded in breaking his original grip.

Slide both arms up under his wrist as you fall back to complete the armbar, remembering to keep the knees and hips tight while keeping his thumb pointed upward.

Technique 108
KEY LOCK WITH LEGS TO BREAK THE DOUBLE-FOREARM GRIP

Your opponent is holding on to both of his forearms with his opposite hands so that you are unable to break your opponent's grip with your arms.

Move your right hip toward his head.

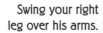

Swing your right leg over his arms.

While holding his arm tightly against your chest with your right arm, you can grab your shin with your other arm.

Let go of your shin when you lock your left leg over your right. As you pull back on his arm, it may cause enough pain to cause him to submit right here.

If not, it will at least put on enough pressure for him to let go of his grip.

Finish the armbar.

Technique 109

TRIANGLE ARMBAR COMBINATION

Once again, you are unable to break your opponent's grip with your arms.

Lean to your right side so you are able to pull you left foot back as if to push his biceps to break his grip.

Instead, slide your left leg under his right arm.

Release your right leg from over his head.

As he lifts up his head to escape, slide your right leg under his head.

Hook your left foot under your right calf.

Cinch the "triangle" tightly around his neck as he attempts to rise.

Drive him down with your legs and pull his arm free with your arms. Straighten your body to apply the triangle armbar combination.

Appendix I:
FINISHING MOVES

NECK CRANK
Technique: 21, 39, 40, 45, 46, 82

KIMURA
Technique: 9, 10, 11, 64, 71

ARMBAR/ARM LOCK
Technique: 5, 12, 14, 15, 16, 31, 35, 42, 59, 60, 62, 65, 87, 92, 93, 94, 95, 97, 98, 102, 104, 108, 109

CONTROL POSITION
Technique: 1, 2, 22

TOEHOLD
Technique: 80

Photo by Greg Wetzel

CHOKE
Technique: 34, 41, 43, 44, 51, 52, 53, 54, 55, 57, 61, 66, 67, 72, 83, 84, 85, 86, 88, 89, 91, 96, 99, 101, 103

SHOULDER LOCK
Technique: 20, 23, 26, 47, 68, 69, 73, 74, 90, 100

ELBOW LOCK
Technique: 3, 4, 6, 7, 8, 13, 17, 18, 19, 24, 25, 28, 29, 30, 32, 33, 49, 50, 58, 63

WRIST LOCK
Technique: 27, 38, 48, 56, 70, 105, 106, 107

KNEE BAR
Technique: 36, 37, 75, 76, 77, 78, 79, 81

Appendix II:
SITUATION-SPECIFIC
TECHNIQUE APPLICATIONS

SIDE-MOUNT CONTROL
Techniques: 1 and 2

When obtaining the side mount, it is important to be able to control your opponent until you can find or make an opening for a submission. The object is to give your opponent no space at any time, unless you are attempting to lure him into a mistake that will provide a submission opening. If you are controlling him in a correct fashion, you will feel heavier and stronger than you really are. Since you may be competing with an opponent of equal or near-equal skill who is adept at escaping your side control, you must be able to change position in order to counter his escapes while still maintaining tight control. Or you may simply find it advantageous to continue your attack from the opposite side.

OPPONENT'S ARM BELOW YOUR HEAD
Techniques: 3, 4, 5, 9, 10, 11, 12, 13, 14, 15, 16, 17, 18, 19, 20, 21, 22, 23, 24, 25, 26, 27, 28, 61 and 62

The position of your opponent's arms often determines which submissions you will be able to attempt. These techniques can be initiated when his lower arm is below your head or on the side of your head that is closer to his legs. Many of the techniques will be logical progressions of the beginning initial technique based on his lower arm's position.

OPPONENT'S ARM ABOVE YOUR HEAD
Techniques: 6, 7, 8, 45, 46, 56, 57, 58, 59 and 60

These techniques can be initiated when the lower arm is above your head or on your upper shoulder that is closest to your opponent's head.

KESA GATAME POSITION
Techniques: 29, 30, 31, 32, 33, 34 and 35

Sometimes you need to go to the *kesa gatame* position in order to keep a wily opponent from escaping. Often, this controlling position is used when your opponent pushes on your hip during your standard side-mount control in order to make space for his escape attempt. (See technique 29 for details on achieving this position.)

HEAD LOCK POSITION
Techniques: 47, 48, 49, 50 and 51

I don't recommend spending too much time in this position against higher skilled opponents since it is relatively easy for them to escape and put you in a bad position. However, in case you end up here in the course of the match, these techniques can be used for submission.

ARM AROUND OPPONENT'S NECK
Techniques: 39, 40, 41, 42, 43 and 44

These submissions have a high percentage of success when your upper arm is under your opponent's neck and controlling his head.

HEAD MOUNT (NORTH/SOUTH)
Techniques: 63, 64, 65, 66, 67, 68, 69, 70, 71, 72, 73 and 74

As your opponent attempts escapes, you may find yourself controlling him from the head-mount position. There are many submissions you can obtain from this position. If you practice and become adept with these techniques, you may become strong enough to intentionally move to this position to secure submissions.

OPPONENT GOES TO HIS KNEES (TURTLE POSITION)
Techniques: 82, 83, 84, 85, 86, 87, 88, 89, 90, 91, 92, 93, 94, 95, 96, 97, 98, 99, 100, 101, 102, 103 and 104

It is common for your opponent to escape to his knees to avoid side control or as a desperate measure to prevent you from passing his guard. These sequences can be used in the event you end up controlling from that position.

MISCELLANEOUS WRIST LOCKS AND CHOKES
Techniques: 38, 52, 53, 54, 55 and 56

These techniques can be applied when your opponent hides his arms. They can also be initiated when your opponent's arms are in various positions.

ATTACKING THE LEGS
Techniques: 36, 37, 75, 76, 77, 78, 79, 80 and 81

It is important to learn to attack the legs, especially after you have mastered many of the upper-body submissions. This will keep your opponent off guard by giving him more things to worry about. Because attacking the legs often means having to give up your dominant position, it is recommended that you attack the legs only when you feel there is a high chance of achieving submission.

SIDE-MOUNT ARMBAR POSITION
TECHNIQUES: 105, 106, 107, 108 AND 109

When attempting an armbar from the side mount, your opponent will do everything he can to prevent you from straightening his arm for the submission. Since you worked hard to earn this dangerous position, these techniques are important tools for breaking the various grips he might use to protect his arm.

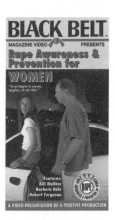

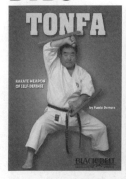